Elimin 8 Plus Corn
Food Allergy Cookbook

Life can be delicious,
free of the 8 most
common food allergens:
dairy, egg, wheat, soy,
peanut, tree nut, fish,
shellfish AND corn

By Betsy Chabin

Elimin 8 Plus Corn
Food Allergy Cookbook
Life can be delicious, free of the 8 most common
food allergens: dairy, egg, wheat, soy, peanut,
tree nut, fish, shellfish AND corn

ISBN 978-0-577-30675-6
Published by Lulu.com
Printed in the United States of America

Disclaimer

While every caution has been taken to provide you with the most honest and accurate information, please use your discretion before making any decisions based on the information in this cookbook. The information provided is based on personal experiences and consults with our physicians and dieticians. It is your responsibility to consult with your doctor and to do what is medically best for you based on your diagnosis. I cannot be responsible for allergic reactions from making use of these recipes. It is your responsibility to check the ingredients in your food and to research unfamiliar words on all products before using them. Please, be label stable!

This book is dedicated to Nathan. Thank you for inspiring our family to have a delicious life together!

This book is also written for other children who struggle with food allergies. Here's to heaping plates of food and eyes that are bigger than your stomachs!

Chabin recipe for life:

1 cup of James' honesty
1 cup of Sarah's enthusiasm
1 cup of Nathan's love
1 cup of John's compassion
1 cup of Betsy's patience

Mix well and live!

Betsy Chabin lives in Tucson, Arizona, where she and her husband are raising their three children. She holds a Bachelors Degree from The University of Arizona, and received her Masters of Social Work from Portland State University. Betsy has spent years collecting and creating safe foods to serve to her family.

Table of Contents

Good Morning!

Breakfast **21**

What's For Dinner?

Main Courses **31**

May I have more?

Side Dishes

Healthy Habits!

Salads

Introduction

Twelve years ago I would have laughed (or cried) at the notion of a home without dairy, egg, wheat, soy, peanut, tree nut, fish, shellfish, corn, chicken and chocolate. It didn't happen all at once, but over the years our family has accumulated these allergies. We have discovered, however, that there is life without these foods and that this life is delicious to live!

It would be an exaggeration to say that our home is completely free of all of these foods. Not all of our family members have the same food allergies. The severity of our food allergies ranges from high to low. Do we all avoid peanuts? Yes, all of us. The peanut allergy is potentially fatal so we have no foods containing peanuts in our home. Regardless of severity, all of the meals I prepare are allergen-free, so each of us can relax and enjoy our food.

One of our children has a condition called Eosinophilic Esophagitis (EE), which our doctor deemed the "mother of all food allergies." Wikipedia tells us that EE is "an allergic inflammatory condition of the esophagus. Symptoms are swallowing difficulty, food impaction, heartburn [and] food allergy may play a significant role."

Treatment for EE begins with the elimination diet. We eliminated the eight most common food allergens from our child's diet: dairy, egg, wheat, soy, peanut, tree nut, fish and shellfish. Our allergist instructed us to eliminate corn, as well. This request was based on his clinical observations that corn allergies are on the rise. Weeks later, upon allergy testing, we discovered our child *is* allergic to corn. Thus, the title of this cookbook: Elimin 8 plus Corn.

After eliminating so many allergens, I felt that our food choices were limited, redundant and difficult to make into dinners and desserts. Over time, with patience and much experimentation, I have discovered numerous recipes that are not only pleasing for the family, but also delicious enough to serve to company.

This cookbook offers typical meals that require very few specialty items. A good health food store and a regular grocery store is all that is needed to find the ingredients used in my recipes.

My goal is to save you time, reduce your stress and to help you enjoy food again. I offer recipes that are easy to make, easy to find and delicious! My wish to you is that you may have peace of mind.

Be Label Stable

Learn to be label stable! Know how to read a label and research the ingredients that are not familiiar to you.

In 2006 a Federal law was passed requiring food manufacturers to label all foods containing a major allergen. Currently, the allergens disclosed are the top eight: dairy, egg, wheat, soy, peanut, tree nut, fish and shellfish.

Food labels are required to show the allergens in, under, or next to the ingredient list. Manufacturers may use different statements so you have to read carefully. For example, a product containing dairy may say: "**allergen information: milk**," or "**contains milk**," or "**milk**." If the manufacturer includes the allergens *in* the list of ingredients, the allergens common name must follow in parenthesis, for example, "**casein (milk).**"

Look up the ingredients that are not familiar to you. For example, "milk" can be represented by some of these words: whey, casein, casinates, lactullose or nisin.

You can visit the FAAN website and download information sheets that will provide you with all of the words associated with the top eight allergens.

Label Stable Tips

Always read the label before purchasing a product.

Re-read the label at home before using a product.

Read the label even if you buy the product all the time: ingredients change.

Look up the words you do not know: the internet has current information.

Ask to see the label of foods used in restaurants.

Read labels on shampoos, soaps, lotions, cosmetics and any other product you use on your skin.

Read labels on toothpaste, mouthwash, mints and chewing gum; they often contain corn derivatives.

Read labels on pet food, they often contain human allergens like peanut butter and cheese.

Baking Tips

Buy rolled oats in bulk. Use a coffee grinder or a blender to grind the oats into oat-flour for baking. Check that the oats are wheat-free.

Hains makes Featherweight Baking Powder, which is made with potato starch rather than cornstarch.

Spectrum brand shortening is organic and made of palm oil.

Most health food stores carry confectioners sugar made with tapioca rather than cornstarch.

Bacon can be bought precooked. It only takes 30 seconds in the microwave!

Allergen-free chocolate chips can be found at most health food stores and several grocery store chains.

If you are having difficulty finding a food that is allergen-free, try looking into organic products.

Iodized salt often contains dextrose (corn), but you can find it in the grocery store without iodide.

Wheat-free chicken, beef and vegetable broth can be found at most health food stores and several grocery store chains.

Replacement Tips

1 cup milk equals	one cup rice milk **or** one cup fruit juice
One cup butter equals	one cup shortening **or** one cup oil
One cup oil equals	one cup applesauce plus 2 T oil
One egg equals	3 T applesauce plus 1 t baking powder **or** ½ mashed banana plus 1 t baking powder **or** 1 T vinegar (use only if there is baking soda in the recipe)

SHOPPING LIST

Knowing what foods to buy can be a time consuming and overwhelming experience. I have created a shopping list based on the recipes, as well as some snack foods, that will get you through your first week. All you need is a local health food store and your regular grocery store.

Remember: be label stable! Read the ingredients on the back of the packaging. Manufacturers change ingredients often, so read the label EVERY time. You are responsible for checking each food listed on this shopping list!

Breakfast Foods:
Rolled oats (buy enough for eating and baking)
Bacon (fresh or precooked)
Rice based cereal
Rice Milk
Lunch:
Lunchmeat (organic has fewer additives)
Sunflower seed butter
Jelly
Rice cakes
Rice bread
Dinner.
Ground beef
Ground turkey
Chicken breasts
Pork loin
Side dishes:
Rice
Rice pasta
Quinoa

Black beans
Green beans
Kidney beans
Diced tomatoes
Tomato sauce
Potatoes
Onions
Veggies
Fruit
Cilantro
Lettuce
Red pepper
Snacks:
Potato chips (check oil used)
Veggie chips
Raisins or other dried fruit
Applesauce
Annie's organic bunny fruit snacks
Desserts:
Sorbet (Amy's)
Natural soda (Hains)
Spices, other
Baking powder (Hains Featherweight)
Garlic
Olive oil
Canola oil
Curry powder
Rice syrup
Honey
Apple cider vinegar
Shortening (Spectrum organic palm oil)

Good Morning!

Breakfast Foods

Quick Potato Bake
Serves 1

1 russet potato, cut into bite sized cubes
1 slice bacon, chopped*
1 tablespoon olive oil
3 tablespoons salsa
Salt and pepper to taste*

Place cubed potato into a microwave safe dish. Stir in olive oil, salsa, bacon, salt and pepper. Place paper towel over the bowl and cook in microwave on high for 3 minutes. Stir; cook 2 more minutes or until potatoes are soft and begin to mash as you stir them. Let cool slightly and serve.

*See baking tips, page 17

Pancakes
12 pancakes

1 cup rice flour*
1 cup oat flour*
2 tablespoons sugar
½ teaspoon cinnamon
2 teaspoons baking powder*
1 teaspoon apple cider vinegar
½ teaspoon salt*
1 cup rice milk
2 tablespoons applesauce
1 tablespoon canola oil

In a mixer or large bowl, combine rice flour, oat flour, sugar, cinnamon, baking powder, salt and vinegar; mix. Add rice milk and stir until mixture has a smooth consistency. Add applesauce and oil; stir.

Scoop batter into an oiled skillet and cook over medium heat. Let pancake cook until it bubbles, then flip and cook the other side.

Add a cup of blueberries to the batter and make blueberry pancakes!

*See baking tips, page 17

Pumpkin Muffins
12 muffins

3 cups oat flour*
1½ cups sugar
½ cup canola oil
1 (15-ounce) can pumpkin
1 teaspoon baking powder*
1 teaspoon baking soda
¼ teaspoon ground cloves
1 teaspoon ground cinnamon
¼ teaspoon ground nutmeg
½ teaspoon salt*
1 tablespoon apple cider vinegar

In a mixer or large bowl, combine flour, sugar, oil and pumpkin; mix well. Add baking powder, baking soda, cloves, cinnamon, nutmeg, salt and vinegar; mix well. Scoop batter into greased or lined muffin cups.

Bake at 350 for 25 minutes.

*See baking tips, page 17

Banana Muffins
12 muffins

3 cups oat flour*
1 cup sugar
½ cup canola oil
1 teaspoon baking powder*
1 teaspoon baking soda
½ teaspoon salt*
1 tablespoon apple cider vinegar
1 cup orange juice
3 ripe bananas, mashed
Topping:
Sugar to taste

In a mixer or large bowl, combine flour, sugar and oil; mix well. Add baking powder, baking soda, salt and vinegar. Add orange juice and bananas; mix well. Scoop into greased or lined muffin cups and fill ¾ full. Sprinkle sugar on top.

Bake at 375 degrees for 20 minutes.

*See baking tips, page 17

Strawberry Muffins
12 muffins

2½ cups oat flour*
¾ cup brown sugar
¼ cup canola oil
½ cup berry applesauce
½ cup rice milk
½ banana, plus ½ teaspoon baking powder
1 teaspoon baking powder*
1 teaspoon baking soda
1 teaspoon ground cinnamon
1 teaspoon vanilla
1 cup strawberries, finely chopped
½ teaspoon salt*
Topping:
2 tablespoons brown sugar
¼ teaspoon ground cinnamon
1 teaspoon shortening*

In a mixer or a large bowl, combine flour, brown sugar, oil, applesauce and rice milk. In a small bowl, mash banana and baking powder together. Add to mixture. Add baking powder, baking soda, cinnamon, vanilla and salt; mix well. Stir in strawberries. Scoop into greased or lined muffin cups.

Topping: using a fork, mix brown sugar, cinnamon and shortening. Sprinkle over the tops of muffins. Bake at 375 degrees for 25 minutes.
Try replacing the strawberries with blueberries. Our family is split over which muffin is best!
*See baking tips, page 17

Morning Glory Muffins
12 muffins

2 cups oat flour*
1 cup sugar
¼ cup canola oil
½ cup applesauce
1 tablespoon ground cinnamon
2 teaspoons baking powder*
½ teaspoon baking soda
½ teaspoon salt*
1 tablespoon apple cider vinegar
1 teaspoon vanilla extract
1 cup carrot, grated
1 apple, chopped
1 cup raisins

In a mixer or large bowl, combine flour, sugar, oil and applesauce; mix well. Add cinnamon, baking powder, baking soda, salt, vinegar and vanilla. Mix in carrots, apples and raisins. Scoop batter into greased or lined muffin cups, filling ¾ full.

Bake at 375 degrees for 20 minutes.

*See baking tips, page 17

Strawberry Banana Smoothie
Serves 1

1 cup frozen strawberries
½ banana
1 cup orange juice or rice milk

In a blender, place frozen strawberries, banana and liquid; blend. Add more liquid as needed for desired thickness. Blend until smooth.

Smoothies are a healthy and filling way to start your day. Frozen fruit makes the smoothie nice and thick, or you can add 1 cup of ice to fresh fruit.

Granola
Serves 6

4 cups rolled oats*
½ cup brown sugar
½ teaspoon salt*
½ teaspoon ground cinnamon
¼ cup canola oil
¼ cup honey
1 teaspoon vanilla
1 cup raisins

In a bowl, mix oats, brown sugar, salt and cinnamon. In a separate bowl, add oil and honey; warm in the microwave for 30 seconds; stir. Add vanilla; stir. Pour oil mixture over the oats. Mix together, making sure all the oats are covered, using hands if necessary. Spread mixture into a 9 x 13 inch baking pan.

Bake at 300 for 40 minutes. Add raisins after granola has cooled.

This is a wonderful breakfast cereal, snack or dessert.

*See baking tips, page 17

Cranberry Apple Cereal Bars
Serves 6

4 cups rice chex type cereal
½ cup dried cranberries
½ cup dried apples
1 tablespoon canola oil
½ cup rice syrup
¼ cup brown sugar

In a large bowl, mix cereal, cranberries and apples; set aside. In a small saucepan, heat oil, rice syrup and brown sugar over medium heat. Bring to a boil and stir for two minutes. Pour mixture over the cereal and mix until evenly coated. In a well-greased 8-inch pan, press mixture firmly down. Let cool and cut into bars or break into chunks.

These bars make a great snack or dessert too!

*See baking tips, page 17

What's For Dinner?

Main Courses

Chicken Lettuce Fajitas
Serves 4-6

4 boneless chicken breasts, sliced lengthwise
1 yellow pepper, sliced
1 red pepper, sliced
1 green pepper, sliced
1 red onion, sliced
Marinade:
½ cup olive oil
¼ cup rice vinegar
1 lime, juiced
½ teaspoon salt*
2 cloves garlic, minced
1 teaspoon dried oregano
¼ teaspoon ground cumin
Pepper to taste
Wraps:
1 head of lettuce, cut in half

Slice chicken, peppers and onion into long strips. In a small bowl, mix oil, vinegar, lime juice, salt, garlic, oregano, cumin and pepper. Place the chicken mixture in a gallon size freezer bag and pour marinade over it. Place in refrigerator from 30 minutes to overnight.
To cook: pour the marinated ingredients into a large frying pan. Cook covered, over medium high heat. Stir occasionally, until chicken is no longer pink in the middle, approximately 10 minutes.

Slice a head of lettuce in half from the base. Carefully pull leaves apart to make "cups." Place fajitas mix in the lettuce and eat like a taco.

Chicken Mushroom Kabobs
Serves 4-6

4 boneless chicken breasts, cut into bite size pieces
2 onions, cut into bite size pieces
20 small mushrooms, whole
Marinade:
½ cup olive oil
3 tablespoons lemon juice
4 cloves garlic, minced
2 tablespoons dried parsley
1 tablespoon dried basil
1 teaspoon salt*
½ teaspoon pepper

Cut chicken breasts and onion into bite size pieces.
Alternate, placing chicken, mushroom and onion on
skewers.

Marinade: combine oil, lemon juice, garlic, parsley,
basil, salt and pepper in a 9 x 13 inch pan. Place
kabobs in marinade and turn to coat. Cover and
place in refrigerator from 30 minutes to overnight.

Remove chicken from pan, reserving marinade.

Broil or grill 12 to 15 minutes, brushing with marinade,
turning once. Heat reserved marinade and serve with
chicken.

*See baking tips, page 17

Chicken Lettuce Wraps
Serves 6

4 boneless chicken breasts, cut into bite size pieces
2 tablespoons olive oil
½ onion, chopped
2 teaspoons garlic, minced
2 tablespoons brown sugar
2 tablespoons rice vinegar
1 teaspoon salt*
1 can water chestnuts, drained and chopped
2 cups mushrooms, chopped
1 head iceberg lettuce

Cut chicken breasts into small bite size pieces. In a large skillet, add oil, onions and garlic; cook over medium high heat for 5 minutes. Add chicken to skillet and cook for approximately 10 minutes, stirring occasionally. Add brown sugar, vinegar and salt; mix well. Add water chestnuts and mushrooms; stir. Cover and reduce heat to a simmer for 5 minutes or until chicken is no longer pink in the middle.

Slice a head of lettuce in half from the base. Carefully pull leaves apart to make "cups." To serve, scoop the chicken mixture into the lettuce and roll up tortilla style.

Want to spice it up? Add a pinch of cayenne pepper!

*See baking tips, page 17

Curry Stir-fry
Serves 6

4 boneless chicken breasts, cut into bite size pieces
½ onion, chopped
½ cup Dijon style mustard
½ cup honey
1 tablespoon curry powder
½ cup chicken broth*
2 celery stalks, chopped
1 red pepper, chopped
½ head broccoli, chopped
1 tablespoon olive oil
4 cups chicken broth* or water
2 cups white rice

Rice: bring 4 cups of broth or water to a boil. Add 2 cups rice; reduce to a simmer. Cover and cook for 20 minutes.

Chicken: cut chicken breasts into bite size pieces. In a large skillet, add olive oil, chicken and onion. Cook over medium high heat, approximately 10 minutes or until chicken is no longer pink in the middle.

Curry: in a bowl, mix mustard, honey, curry and ½ cup of broth. Pour curry mix over the chicken; stir. Add celery, red pepper and broccoli. Cover and simmer until veggies are steamed to a desirable texture, approximately 10 minutes. Serve curry over rice.

*See baking tips, page 17

Sesame Chicken Salad
Serves 4-5

1 pound chicken tenders
½ cup Dijon style mustard
½ cup honey
1 cup sesame seeds
Dressing:
¼ cup canola oil
2 tablespoons lemon juice
¼ teaspoon ground ginger
1 tablespoon Dijon style mustard
1 tablespoon honey
Salad:
1 bag of mixed greens
½ cucumber, sliced
2 tomatoes, sliced

Chicken: in a small bowl, mix mustard and honey. Place chicken tenders in a gallon size freezer bag. Pour marinade over chicken, refrigerate and let sit from 30 minutes to overnight.

Roll chicken in sesame seeds and bake at 400 degrees for 20 minutes.

Dressing: in a small bowl, combine oil, lemon juice, ginger, mustard and honey.

Salad: in a large bowl, mix lettuce, cucumber and tomato; toss together with dressing. Slice chicken into long strips and place on top of salad. Serve.

Curried Chicken
Serves 4-5

4 chicken breasts
½ cup Dijon style mustard
½ cup honey
2 teaspoons curry powder

Mix mustard, honey and curry powder. Place chicken in a gallon size freezer bag and pour marinade over the top. Place in the refrigerator and let marinate from 30 minutes to overnight.

Bake at 425 for 40 minutes.

Drizzle the extra marinade over rice or potatoes as a side dish. This is a delicious marinade for a cut fryer as well.

Grilled Pork Roast
Serves 4-5

1 pork loin
3 tablespoons olive oil
2 cloves garlic, minced

Place pork in a gallon size freezer bag and pour olive oil and garlic over the top. Place in the refrigerator and let marinate from 30 minutes to overnight.

Oil the grill and place pork over medium high heat. Grill for 15 minutes on one side, turn and grill for another 15 minutes.

Baked Pork Chops with Apples
Serves 4

4 one-inch thick pork chops
2 Granny Smith apples halved and cored
Pepper to taste
Salt to taste*
1 cup brown sugar

Place pork chops in a baking dish. Sprinkle with salt and pepper. Place one apple half; cut side down, on each chop. Sprinkle generously with brown sugar.

Bake uncovered at 350 for 30 minutes.

Save juices to pour over chops.

*See baking tips, page 17

Shredded Pork in Crock Pot
Serves 4-5

1 pork loin
1 (4-ounce) can mild green chiles, chopped
3 cloves garlic, minced
½ teaspoon salt*
½ cup water
Rice:
3 cups water
1½ cups white rice
¼ cup lime juice
¼ cup fresh cilantro, chopped

Place the pork in a crock-pot and sprinkle salt, green chiles and garlic over the top. Pour ½ cup water into the bottom of the crock-pot. Cover and cook on low for 7 hours.

Rice: bring 3 cups of water to a boil. Add lime juice, cilantro and rice. Reduce heat to low, cover and simmer for 20 minutes.

When pork is done, use two forks to shred. Serve over the cooked rice.

Put the pork in the crock-pot in the morning; dinner is ready by 5 p.m!

*See baking tips, page 17

BBQ Ribs
Serves 5

1 (3-pound) rack of ribs
1 tablespoon ground cumin
1 tablespoon chili powder
1 tablespoon ground paprika
¼ teaspoon cayenne pepper
½ teaspoon salt*
½ cup barbeque sauce

In a small bowl, combine cumin, chili powder, paprika, cayenne pepper and salt. Trim the membrane from the back of each rib. Rub the dry mixture over the front and back of the ribs.

Oil the top rack of grill and place foil on the lower rack to catch any drippings. Preheat grill on high for 5 minutes.

Reduce heat to low and lay ribs on the top rack of grill. Let cook for 1½ hours, over low heat.

After cooking for 1½ hours, brush barbeque sauce over the front and back of ribs and let cook 5 more minutes. Serve.

Look for allergen-free barbeque sauce at the health food stores.

See baking tips, page 17

Ground Turkey and Rice
Serves 4-5

1 pound ground turkey
1 onion, chopped
1 teaspoon salt*
Pepper to taste
Rice:
3 cups chicken broth,* or water
1½ cups white rice
2 tablespoons dried basil
1 clove garlic, minced
¼ teaspoon salt*

Rice: in a medium size saucepan, bring 3 cups of chicken broth to a boil. Add rice, basil, garlic and salt; reduce heat to low. Cover and let simmer for 20 minutes.

Turkey: in a skillet, brown turkey and onions over medium high heat for approximately 10 minutes or until turkey is no longer pink in the middle. Drain fat. Sprinkle in salt and pepper.

Serve turkey over rice.

*See baking tips, page 17

Turkey Breast in Crock Pot
Serves 5-6

1 (3-pound) turkey breast half, bone in
1 teaspoon dried garlic
4 tablespoons dried onion flakes
¼ teaspoon lemon pepper
½ teaspoon salt*
4 russet potatoes, quartered
4 large carrots, quartered
1 cup beef broth*

In a small bowl, combine garlic, onion flakes, lemon pepper and salt. Rub mixture onto turkey breast, over and under the skin. Place the quartered potatoes and carrots on the bottom of the crock pot. Place the seasoned turkey breast on top of them. Pour ½ cup of the beef broth over the potatoes and ½ cup over top of turkey breast.

Cook on low for 8 hours.

*See baking tips, page 17

Taco Salad
Serves 5

1 pound ground turkey
½ onion, chopped
2 cloves garlic, minced
1 (15-ounce) can diced tomatoes
2 tablespoons chili powder
1 tablespoon dried oregano
1 teaspoon ground cumin
½ teaspoon salt*
Pepper to taste
Salad:
1 head of fresh lettuce
1 (15-ounce) can black olives, drained
1 (15-ounce) can black beans, rinsed and drained
1 avocado, chopped

In a large skillet, brown turkey, onions and garlic over medium heat approximately 10 minutes or until turkey is no longer pink inside. Drain fat. Add diced tomatoes, chili powder, oregano, cumin, salt and pepper. Bring to a boil; reduce to simmer for approximately 5 minutes. While simmering, prepare your salad.

Salad: cut lettuce into strips or squares. Place lettuce into a large salad bowl. Add olives, beans and avocado; toss. Add ground turkey mixture; toss. Serve in large portions on plates or in bowls.

*See baking tips, page 17

Chili
Serves 6

1 pound ground beef or turkey
1 medium onion, chopped
1 (15-ounce) can diced tomatoes
1 (15-ounce) can tomato sauce (save can to refill)
1 refilled can water
1 clove garlic, crushed
1 bay leaf
¼ teaspoon cayenne pepper (or to taste)
1 teaspoon oregano
1 teaspoon ground cumin
1 teaspoon salt*
1 tablespoon chili powder
2 (15-ounce) cans kidney beans, drained
Pepper to taste

In a large stockpot, brown beef and onions over medium high heat approximately 10 minutes or until beef is no longer pink in the middle. Drain fat. Add diced tomatoes, tomato sauce, water, garlic, bay leaf, cayenne pepper, oregano, cumin, salt and chili powder. Bring to a boil then reduce to a simmer. Add kidney beans and let simmer for 30 minutes.

The cayenne pepper can really add a kick, you may want to start with 1/8 teaspoon and slowly add more.

*See baking tips, page 17

Eggplant Casserole
Serves 6

1 pound ground beef
1 onion, chopped
2 cloves garlic, minced
1 (15-ounce) can tomato sauce
1 (15-ounce) can diced tomatoes
3 tablespoons dried parsley
1 teaspoon dried thyme
1 teaspoon dried oregano
1 teaspoon dried basil
1 eggplant

In a large skillet, brown beef, onion and garlic over medium high heat. Drain fat. Add tomato sauce, diced tomatoes, parsley, thyme, oregano and basil; stir. Let simmer for 10 minutes. Slice eggplant into thin rounds. In a 9 x 13 baking dish, place a layer of eggplant, followed by a layer of ground beef mixture. Repeat the layers until the eggplant slices and the ground beef mixtures are gone.

Cover with foil and bake at 350 degrees for one hour. Remove foil and bake for another 20 minutes.

Spaghetti with Rice Pasta
Serves 4-5

1 pound ground beef
2 cloves garlic, minced
1 (15-ounce) can tomato sauce
1 (15-ounce) can diced tomatoes
1 tablespoon dried oregano
½ teaspoon dried basil
½ cup fresh cilantro, chopped
1 pound rice pasta, spaghetti style

Cook rice pasta according to package directions.

In a skillet, brown beef and garlic over medium high heat approximately 10 minutes or until beef is no longer pink inside. Drain fat. Add tomato sauce, diced tomatoes, garlic, oregano, basil and cilantro; stir. Bring mixture to a boil; reduce heat to a simmer for 10 minutes.

Serve sauce over pasta.

Penne With Sausage
Serves 4-5

½ pound ground Italian sausage
3 cloves garlic, minced
½ onion, chopped
1 (28-ounce) can tomato sauce
½ cup dry red wine or water
1 (7-ounce) jar roasted red peppers
1 cup fresh mustard greens, chopped
1 pound rice pasta, penne style

Cook rice pasta according to package directions.

In a large skillet, cook sausage, garlic and onion over medium high heat for approximately 10 minutes or until sausage is no longer pink inside. Drain fat. Add tomato sauce, wine, red peppers and mustard greens. Bring to a boil; reduce heat to low and simmer for 10 minutes.

Serve sauce over pasta.

Beef Soup
Serves 5

1 pound ground beef
1 onion, chopped
6 cups beef broth*
3 stalks of celery, chopped
2 carrots, sliced
1 (15-ounce) can green beans, drained
1 (15-ounce) can tomato sauce (save can to refill)
1 refilled can water
½ teaspoon salt*
1 teaspoon pepper

In a stockpot, brown beef and onions over medium high heat, approximately 10 minutes or until beef is no longer pink inside. Drain fat. Add broth, celery, carrots, green beans, tomato sauce, salt and pepper. Refill empty tomato sauce can with water and add to soup; stir. Bring to a boil; reduce heat to low. Let simmer for 30 minutes.

*See baking tips, page 17

Lentil and Sausage Soup
Serves 5

1 pound ground sausage
1 onion, chopped
1 carrot, sliced
1 green bell pepper, diced
2 cloves garlic, crushed
1 bay leaf
¼ teaspoon dried thyme
6 cups chicken broth*
1 (15-ounce) can diced tomatoes (save can to refill)
1 refilled can water
1 ¼ cup dried lentils
½ teaspoon salt*
¼ teaspoon pepper

In a stockpot, brown sausage and onions over medium high heat, approximately 10 minutes, or until sausage is no longer pink inside. Drain fat. Reduce heat to medium; add carrots, green peppers, garlic, bay leaf and thyme; cook for 5 minutes. Add broth, tomatoes, water, lentils, salt and pepper; bring to a boil. Reduce heat, cover and simmer for 1 hour.

See baking tips, page 17

Minestrone Soup
Serves 6

½ pound bacon*
1 onion, chopped
3 cloves garlic, crushed
2 celery stalks, chopped
1 (15-ounce) can tomato sauce
6 cups chicken broth*
1 (15-ounce) can kidney beans, drained
1 (15-ounce) can white beans, drained
2 carrots, sliced
1 teaspoon dried basil
1 teaspoon dried oregano
1 bay leaf
1½ cups seashell shaped rice pasta

Chop bacon into bite size pieces. In a stockpot, over
medium heat, cook bacon, onion, garlic and celery
until soft. Add tomato sauce, chicken broth, beans,
carrots, basil, oregano and bay leaf. Bring to a boil
over medium high heat; cover and reduce heat to low;
simmer for 20 minutes. Add pasta; cover and
continue simmering until shells are soft, approximately
30 minutes.

*See baking tips, page 17

Barley and Beef Soup
Serves 6

1 pound ground beef
1 onion, chopped
2 cloves garlic, crushed
2 carrots, sliced
2 cups mushrooms, sliced
6 cups chicken broth*
1 cup water
¼ teaspoon dried thyme
1 bay leaf
3 tablespoons dried parsley
½ teaspoon salt*
½ teaspoon pepper
1 cup pearl barley

In a stockpot, brown beef and onions over medium high heat for approximately 10 minutes or until beef is no longer pink inside. Drain fat. Add garlic, carrots and mushrooms; cook for 5 minutes. Add broth, water, thyme, bay leaf, parsley, salt, pepper and barley. Bring to a boil then reduce heat to low. Cover and let simmer for one hour or until barley is tender.

*See baking tips, page 17

Vegetable Soup
Serves 6

½ pound ground turkey
1 onion, chopped
1 green pepper, chopped
4 carrots, sliced
4 cups chicken broth*
1 (15-ounce) can tomato sauce (save can to refill)
1 refilled can of water
1 teaspoon dried basil
1 teaspoon dried oregano
1 teaspoon salt*
5 small potatoes, cut into chunks
½ head cauliflower, cut into chunks
1 zucchini, sliced

In a stockpot, over medium high heat, brown turkey
and onions until turkey is no longer pink inside,
approximately 10 minutes. Drain fat. Add green
peppers, carrots, broth, tomato sauce, water, basil,
oregano and salt. Bring to a boil. Reduce heat to low
and add potatoes, cauliflower and zucchini. Cover
and let simmer for several hours.

*See baking tips, page 17

Peppered Flank Steak
Serves 5-6

2 flank steaks, approximately 2 pounds each
Marinade:
½ cup olive oil
½ cup rice vinegar
¼ cup Dijon style mustard
4 cloves garlic, minced
4 green onion sprigs, chopped
1 tablespoon black pepper
1 teaspoon dried thyme
1 teaspoon dried rosemary
1 teaspoon salt*

Marinade: in a small bowl, add oil, vinegar, mustard, garlic, onion, pepper, thyme, rosemary and salt; stir.

Place flank steaks into a gallon size freezer bag and pour marinade over the steaks. Refrigerate and let marinate from 30 minutes to overnight.

Oil the grill and place steaks over medium high heat. Grill for 15 minutes on each side, or until the meat is cooked to your preference.

*See baking tips, page 17

May I have more?

Side Dishes

Spicy Beans and Rice
Serves 4-6

1 tablespoon canola oil
½ onion, chopped
½ green pepper, chopped
2 cloves garlic, minced
1 (15-ounce) can diced tomatoes
1 (15-ounce) can black beans, drained
1 cup water
1 teaspoon chili powder
¼ teaspoon cayenne pepper
½ teaspoon salt*
2/3 cup rice

In a large skillet, add oil, onion, green pepper and garlic; cook over medium high heat until tender. Stir in diced tomatoes, black beans, water, chili powder, cayenne pepper and salt. Stir in uncooked rice and bring to a boil.

Transfer into a baking dish and bake at 375 degrees for ½ hour; remove and stir; place back in oven for another ½ hour.

My kids love this dish served with a dollop of guacamole on top!

*See baking tips, page 17

Calico Beans
Serves 4-6

6 bacon strips, chopped*
1 onion, chopped
2 cloves garlic, minced
¾ cup brown sugar
½ cup catsup
1 teaspoon salt*
1 teaspoon dry mustard
2 teaspoons apple cider vinegar
1 (15-ounce) can kidney beans, drained
1 (15-ounce) can green beans, drained
1 (15-ounce) can navy beans, drained
1 (15-ounce) can baked beans, drained

In a saucepan over medium-high heat, brown bacon, onion and garlic; cook until tender, approximately 5 minutes. Stir in brown sugar, catsup, salt, mustard and vinegar. Add drained beans; mix well. Transfer into a baking dish.

Bake at 350 for 40 minutes.

This is a great recipe for potlucks!

*See baking tips, page 17

Chinese Rice
Serves 4-6

2 cups white rice
1 (15-ounce) can peas, drained
1½ cups celery, chopped
½ onion, chopped
1 (8-ounce) can water chestnuts, drained
1 (4-ounce) can mushrooms, drained
Dressing
½ cup canola oil
1 tablespoon celery seed
1 clove garlic, minced
3 teaspoons apple cider vinegar
1 teaspoon salt*
½ teaspoon sugar
2 teaspoons curry powder

Bring 4 cups of water to a boil. Add 2 cups rice and chopped onion. Cover; reduce heat to a simmer for 20 minutes. After rice is cooked, add peas, celery, onion, water chestnuts and mushrooms; mix well.

Dressing: in a small bowl, mix oil, celery seed, garlic, vinegar, salt, sugar and curry. Pour dressing over cooked rice mixture; mix well. Serve hot or cold.

*See baking tips, page 17

Basil Rice
Serves 4-6

3 cups chicken broth*
1½ cups white rice
2 tablespoons dried basil
1 clove garlic, minced
¼ teaspoon salt*

Bring broth to a boil. Add rice, basil, garlic and salt;
stir. Cover; reduce heat to a simmer and cook for 20
minutes. Serve.

*See baking tips, page 17

Mashed Potatoes
Serves 4-6

4 cups chicken broth*
2 cups water
6 large russet potatoes, peeled and cut into quarters
¼ cup olive oil
1 teaspoon dried chives
1 teaspoon salt*
Pepper to taste
Reserved liquid

Bring 4 cups of broth plus 2 cups of water to a boil. Reduce heat to medium and place potatoes in the broth; cook for approximately 20 minutes. When the potatoes are soft enough to pierce with a fork, drain, reserving the liquid. Add oil, 1 cup of reserved liquid, chives, salt and pepper; mash. Add reserved liquid as needed for moisture.

Try using a mixer and whip the potatoes!

*See baking tips, page 17

Oven Potatoes
Serves 4-6

8 red potatoes, quartered
¼ cup olive oil
½ teaspoon sea salt*
Pepper to taste

Place quartered potatoes in a large bowl. Pour olive oil and salt over potatoes; mix until potatoes are well covered with oil. Add pepper to taste. Place the potatoes in a baking pan.

Bake at 450 for 15 minutes; turn potatoes. Bake an additional 15 minutes or until potatoes are crispy on the outside and soft on the inside.

*See baking tips, page 17

French Fries
Serves 4-6

5 russet potatoes
¼ cup olive oil
½ teaspoon salt*
¼ teaspoon paprika
Pepper to taste

Slice potatoes in half, lengthwise; cut each half into six or more wedges, depending on the desired thickness of fries. Place fries in a bowl and coat them with olive oil, salt and pepper. Using the oil mixture, grease the baking pan and place fries in a single layer; sprinkle with paprika.

Bake at 425 degrees for 15 minutes, flip fries and bake for an additional 15 minutes, or until crispy on the outside, soft on the inside.

*See baking tips, page 17

Sesame Asparagus
Serves 4-6

1 bunch asparagus, chopped
4 tablespoons olive oil
1 tablespoon sugar
1 tablespoon sesame seeds

Chop asparagus into bite size pieces. In a skillet,
add oil and asparagus. Cover and heat on high for
2 minutes; stir in sesame seeds and sprinkle with
sugar; cook for one minute. Serve immediately.

Grilled Squash
Serves 4-6

¼ cup olive oil
1 clove garlic, minced
2 zucchini squash, cut in chunks
1 yellow squash, cut in chunks
1 red pepper, sliced

In a medium bowl, mix the olive oil and garlic. Place squash and red peppers in the bowl; stir until well covered with oil. Transfer the vegetables to a large piece of foil; fold the edges together forming a pouch. Place on the top rack of the grill over medium high heat.

Grill squash for 10 minutes. Open the foil, and grill for another 10 minutes. When they reach desired tenderness, remove from grill and serve.

Try different vegetables, they all taste great.

Healthy Habits!

Salads

Artichoke Rice Salad
Serves 4-6

1½ cups rice
1 (8-ounce) can water-packed artichoke hearts,
drained and quartered.
1 tomato, diced
1 (15-ounce) can olives, drained
Dressing
½ cup olive oil
¼ cup rice vinegar
¼ cup green onion, chopped
3 cloves garlic, minced
1 tablespoon dried basil
1 teaspoon dried dill

Cook rice according to package directions. Let rice
cool.

In a large bowl, add artichoke hearts, diced tomato
and olives. Add rice; mix well.

Dressing: in a small bowl, mix oil, vinegar, onion,
garlic, basil and dill. Pour dressing over rice salad
and stir until rice is well coated. Chill and serve.

*This salad is great for a picnic or potluck. It tastes
even better on the second day!*

Coleslaw
Serves 4-6

1 head cabbage, shredded
2 carrots, shredded
½ onion, chopped
1 cup dried cranberries
¾ cup sugar
1 tablespoon warm water
Dressing
½ cup apple cider vinegar
¼ cup canola oil
1 teaspoon celery seed
1 teaspoon sugar
Salt to taste

Dressing: in a saucepan, bring vinegar, canola oil, celery seed, sugar and salt to a boil over medium high heat; set aside and let cool.

In a large bowl, combine cabbage, carrots, onion, cranberries, sugar and water. Toss and let sit until the sugar has dissolved.

Pour cooled dressing over cabbage; toss. Refrigerate.

Quinoa Salad
Serves 4-6

2 cups water
1 clove garlic, minced
1 cup quinoa
1 (15-ounce) can black beans, drained
1 red pepper, diced
1 tomato, diced
Dressing:
3 tablespoons olive oil
1 lime, juiced
½ teaspoon cumin
¼ teaspoon salt
Pepper to taste

Bring 2 cups of water to a boil. Reduce heat; add quinoa and garlic; cover and simmer for 15 minutes.

Let cooked quinoa cool slightly. Add beans, red pepper and tomato; toss.

Dressing: in a small bowl, mix olive oil, lime juice, cumin, salt and pepper.

Pour dressing over the quinoa; mix well. Serve hot or cold.

*See baking tips, page 17

Black Bean Salad
Serves 4-6

1 (15-ounce) can black beans, drained
1 green pepper, chopped
1 carrot, grated
1 tablespoon onion, finely chopped
Dressing
2 tablespoons canola oil
3 tablespoons lime juice
¼ teaspoon cumin
1 clove garlic, minced
¼ teaspoon pepper
¼ teaspoon salt*

In a large bowl, combine beans, green pepper, carrot and onion.

Dressing: in a small bowl, mix oil, lime juice, cumin, garlic, pepper and salt.

Pour dressing over bean salad; toss. Serve cold.

*See baking tips, page 17

Three Bean Salad
Serves 4-6

1 (15-ounce) can green beans, drained
1 (15-ounce) can garbanzo beans, drained
1 (15-ounce) can kidney beans, drained
1 onion, chopped
1 red pepper, chopped
Dressing:
½ cup canola oil
½ cup apple cider vinegar
½ cup sugar
1 teaspoon salt*
Pepper to taste

Place drained beans in a large bowl. Add onion and red peppers; stir.

Dressing: in a small bowl combine oil, vinegar, sugar, salt and pepper.

Pour dressing over the bean mixture; toss. Chill and serve.

*See baking tips, page 17

Spinach Salad
Serves 4-6

1 bundle of rinsed spinach, or 1 package of ready-to-eat spinach
½ red onion, chopped
1 (11-ounce) can mandarin oranges, drained
1 cup raisins
Dressing:
¼ cup canola oil
¼ cup water
¼ cup sugar
¼ cup apple cider vinegar

Place spinach in a large salad bowl; add onion, oranges and raisins; toss.

Dressing: in a small bowl, mix oil, water, sugar and vinegar. Pour dressing over salad; toss. Serve.

Sweet and Sour Poppy Seed Salad
Serves 4-6

1 head rinsed romaine lettuce, or 1 ready-to-eat
package of romaine lettuce
1 cup fresh mushrooms, sliced
½ red onion, thinly sliced
1 tomato, sliced
1 carrot, shredded
½ cup dried cranberries
6 slices of bacon,* cooked and chopped
Dressing:
¼ cup lime juice
½ cup honey
½ teaspoon poppy seed
½ teaspoon dry mustard
¼ teaspoon salt*
½ cup canola oil

In a large bowl, add lettuce, mushrooms, onion,
tomato, carrot, cranberries and bacon; toss together.

Dressing: in a blender or food processor, place lime
juice, honey, poppy seed, dry mustard and salt; blend
well. On low speed, gradually pour in oil, scraping
sides as needed. Pour dressing over salad; toss.
Serve.

*See baking tips, page 17

Fruit Salad

Serves 4-6

½ watermelon, cut into bite size pieces
½ cantaloupe, cut into bite size pieces
1 large bunch of grapes
1 (15-ounce) can pineapple chunks, drained
1 cup fresh blueberries
Any other fruit

Cut fruit into bite sized pieces. In a large bowl, combine watermelon, cantaloupe, grapes, pineapple and blueberries; toss.

Chill and serve.

I grew up eating this fruit salad! My mother uses a melon baller on the watermelon and crinkle cutter on the cantaloupe. It makes the salad look beautiful!

Sparkling Lemon-Lime Jello
Serves 4-6

1 (6-ounce) package lemon jello
2 cups water
1 can Hansen's lime soda (or similar flavor)
1 (20-ounce) can crushed pineapple, drained
1 banana, sliced

Pour jello into a medium size bowl; add 2 cups of boiling water; stir until jello is dissolved. Let cool for five minutes. Add can of soda, drained pineapple, and sliced banana.

Place in the refrigerator until firm.

Jello is a satisfying side dish, snack or dessert! This recipe can be made with any flavor jello, but our favorite is lemon.

Cranberry Jello
Serves 4-6

1 (6-ounce) package of black cherry jello
2 cups water
1 (15-ounce) can whole cranberry sauce
1 (20-ounce) can crushed pineapple, undrained

Pour jello into a medium size bowl; add 2 cups of boiling water; stir until jello is dissolved. Add pineapple with juice and cranberry sauce; mix well.

Place in the refrigerator until firm.

This makes a great addition to Thanksgiving dinner.

Dress it up!

Salad Dressings

Italian Dressing

1 cup canola oil
½ cup apple cider vinegar
1 tablespoon lemon juice
2 cloves garlic, minced
2 tablespoons sugar
½ teaspoon dry mustard
1 teaspoon dried oregano
¼ teaspoon dried dill
1 teaspoon dried basil
Salt* to taste
Pepper to taste

Combine oil, vinegar, lemon, garlic, sugar, mustard, oregano, dill, basil, salt and pepper. Pour into a jar or container. Cover tightly; shake. Store in refrigerator.

French Dressing

1 cup sugar
2 tablespoons dry mustard
2 teaspoons salt
½ onion, chopped
½ cup rice vinegar
2 cups canola oil
3 tablespoons catsup
2 tablespoons celery seed

In a food processor or blender, mix sugar, mustard, salt, onion and vinegar. Gradually add oil. Add catsup and celery seed. Pour into a jar or container. Store in refrigerator.

Poppy Seed Dressing

½ cup lime juice
½ cup honey
1 teaspoon poppy seed
1 teaspoon dry mustard
½ teaspoon salt*
1 cup canola oil

Place all ingredients, except oil, in a blender or food processor; mix well. With the blender on low speed, gradually pour in oil, scraping sides as needed. Pour into a jar or container and store in refrigerator. Shake well before using.

*See baking tips, page 17

Something To Hold Me Over!

Snacks
&
Appetizers

Rice Bread "Tortilla Chips"

4 slices of rice bread
¼ cup olive oil
1 clove garlic, crushed
Salt to taste*

In a small bowl, add olive oil and garlic; stir. Place rice bread on a cookie sheet and brush both sides generously with the oil mixture. Lightly salt one side of bread.

Set oven to broil. Broil bread for approximately 1 minute, or until brown and crispy; turn and broil the other side. Remove from oven. Cut bread diagonally across, then diagonally across the other way. Cut two more times for smaller "chips."

Serve with salsa or hummus!

*See baking tips, page 17

Hummus

1 (15-ounce) can garbanzo beans, drained, reserving
liquid
2 tablespoons lemon juice
2 cloves garlic, crushed
2 tablespoons olive oil
½ teaspoon ground cumin
¼ teaspoon salt*

Drain beans, reserving the liquid. Using a food
processor or blender, add beans, lemon juice,
garlic, olive oil, cumin and salt; blend. Add reserved
liquid as needed for creamy texture.

*Serve the hummus with fresh carrots and rice
crackers.*

*See baking tips, page 17

Salsa

1 (15-ounce) can whole peeled tomatoes, drained
½ onion
½ cup fresh cilantro
1 jalapeno pepper slice (or to taste)

In a blender, add tomatoes, onion, cilantro and
jalapeno pepper; blend.

Not spicy enough? Add another jalapeno slice.

Peach Salsa

2 peaches
¼ onion, finely chopped
½ cup fresh cilantro, chopped
1 jalapeno slice, finely chopped
2 tablespoons lemon or lime juice
Pinch of sugar

Dip the peaches into boiling water for 30 seconds.
Remove skin (it should slide off). Cut peaches into
bite sized pieces. Add onion, cilantro, jalapeno,
lemon and sugar. Stir and chill.

*For mango salsa, substitute the peach with mango
(no need to boil the mango, just peel skin with knife
and slice the mango).*

Easy Guacamole

2 avocados
2 tablespoons salsa
1 tablespoon lime juice

Slice avocados in half; remove seeds and scoop avocado from the shells. Add salsa and lime juice. Mash ingredients together with a fork, serving either chunky or smooth.

Layered Bean Dip

1 (15-ounce) can refried beans
1 cup salsa, divided into ½ cups
¼ cup green onion, chopped
1 (15-ounce) can black olives, sliced
1 avocado, chopped
½ head lettuce, shredded

Mix refried beans with ½ cup salsa. Spread over the bottom of a pan or square dish. Sprinkle chopped onions on top of bean mixture. Next, layer the black olives, then ½ cup salsa, then avocado. Spread the lettuce on top as the final layer. Chill and serve.

Serve with rice bread tortilla chips and fresh vegetables.

"SB&J" Rice Cakes

2 rice cakes
2 tablespoons sunflower seed butter
2 tablespoons grape jelly

Spread one tablespoon sunflower seed butter onto each rice cake. Spread one tablespoon grape jelly on top.

Try sunflower seed butter, brown sugar and sliced bananas!

Turkey Wraps

Turkey breast lunch meat, sliced
Roasted red peppers, thinly sliced
Pickle spears, thinly sliced
1 small can olives, sliced
1 head of lettuce
Dressing:
¼ cup Dijon style mustard
1 tablespoon honey
½ teaspoon curry powder

Dressing: in a small bowl, combine mustard, honey and curry.

Cut lettuce in half from the base and gently pry leaves apart to make "cups." Place one slice of turkey, one slice of red pepper, one slice of pickle and several slices of olive in the lettuce cup; drizzle dressing over the top. Roll lettuce, tucking the ends, burrito style. Insert a toothpick to hold together.

These are a good for lunch and in lunch boxes.

Desserts

Pumpkin Cake
Serves 6-8

2½ cups oat flour*
1 cup sugar
½ cup brown sugar
¼ teaspoon baking powder*
1 teaspoon baking soda
½ teaspoon salt*
½ teaspoon ground nutmeg
½ teaspoon ground cinnamon
¼ teaspoon ground cloves
1 cup canned pumpkin
1 tablespoon apple cider vinegar
1/3 cup canola oil

In a large bowl or mixer, combine flour, sugar, brown sugar, baking powder, baking soda, salt, nutmeg, cinnamon and cloves. Add pumpkin, vinegar and oil; mix well. Pour into a greased 8-inch baking pan.

Bake at 300 degrees for 50 minutes.

This tastes like pumpkin pie and can serve as a substitute on Thanksgiving!

*See baking tips, page 17

Autumn Apple Cake
Serves 6-8

4 cups oat flour*
1 cup sugar
¾ cup canola oil
½ cup applesauce
2 teaspoons ground cinnamon
1 teaspoon ground nutmeg
1 teaspoon salt*
1 teaspoon baking soda
1 teaspoon baking powder
1 tablespoon apple cider vinegar
2 teaspoons vanilla
1 apple, peeled and chopped
1 cup raisins

In a large bowl or mixer, combine flour, sugar, oil and applesauce. Add cinnamon, nutmeg, salt, baking soda, baking powder, vinegar and vanilla; mix well. Mix in apple and raisins. Pour into a greased 8-inch baking pan.

Bake at 350 degrees for 40 minutes.

To make into bars, pour batter into a greased 9 x 13 inch baking pan, bake at 350 for 35 minutes.

*See baking tips, page 17

Berry Granola "Cobbler"
Serves 6

¼ cup brown sugar
¼ teaspoon ground ginger
¼ teaspoon allspice
2 cups fresh or frozen blueberries
1 cup fresh or frozen strawberries, sliced
Topping:
2 cups rolled oats
¼ cup brown sugar
¼ teaspoon salt*
¼ teaspoon ground cinnamon
2 tablespoons canola oil
2 tablespoons honey
½ teaspoon vanilla

In a medium size bowl, combine brown sugar, ginger and allspice. Add blueberries and strawberries; toss and let sit.

Topping: in a bowl, mix oats, brown sugar, salt and cinnamon. In a separate bowl, add oil and honey; warm in the microwave for 30 seconds; stir. Add vanilla; stir. Pour oil mixture over the oats. Mix together, making sure all the oats are covered, using hands if necessary. Place berry mix in a baking dish and spread topping over and around the berries.

Bake at 300 for 35 minutes.

*See baking tips, page 17

Apple Butter Crumb Bars
Serves 6-8

2 cups oat flour*
1 cup brown sugar
1 teaspoon baking soda
½ teaspoon ground cinnamon
2½ cups rolled oats
1 cup shortening*
1½ cups apple butter

In a large bowl, combine flour, sugar, baking soda, cinnamon and oats. With a pastry blender or 2 knives, cut in shortening until mixture is crumbly. Spread half the oat mixture evenly over the bottom of an ungreased 9 x 13 inch baking pan and press down lightly. Spread apple butter evenly over the crumb layer. Sprinkle remaining oat mixture over the top, pressing down lightly.

Bake at 400 degrees for 25 minutes. Let cool 15 minutes before cutting into squares.

*See baking tips, page 17

Chocolate Sauce

2 cups sugar
2 tablespoons rice syrup
1 cup water
¾ cup unsweetened cocoa
2 teaspoons vanilla

In a medium size saucepan, add sugar, rice syrup, water and cocoa; stir. Bring to a boil over medium heat. Let mixture boil for three minutes, stirring constantly. Let cool. Add vanilla; stir.

Store in a jar or container in the refrigerator.

This is great drizzled over sorbet!

You can also add a few tablespoons to rice milk and have chocolate milk or hot cocoa.

Try dipping a banana or strawberry in the chocolate sauce!

Chocolate Devils Food Cake
Serves 6-8

2 cups oat flour*
½ cup sugar
½ cup canola oil
1 cup applesauce
½ cup cocoa powder
½ teaspoon baking soda
½ teaspoon salt*
1 tablespoon apple cider vinegar
½ cup semi-sweet chocolate chips
Topping:
½ cup oat flour*
¼ cup sugar
3 tablespoons canola oil
½ cup semi-sweet chocolate chips

In a large bowl or mixer, add flour, sugar, oil and applesauce; mix. Add cocoa, baking soda, salt and vinegar; mix. Stir in chocolate chips. Spread into a greased 8-inch baking pan.

Topping: mix together oat flour, sugar, canola oil and chocolate chips; sprinkle evenly over the top of cake.

Bake at 350 for 30 minutes.

Try this with chocolate frosting, page 105.

*See baking tips, page 17

Carrot Cake
Serves 6-8

2½ cups oat flour*
1½ cups sugar
1 cup applesauce
½ cup rice milk
1 teaspoon baking powder*
2 teaspoons baking soda
½ teaspoon salt*
1 tablespoon ground cinnamon
¼ teaspoon ground cloves
½ teaspoon ground nutmeg
2 tablespoons apple cider vinegar
1½ teaspoons vanilla
1 (8-ounce) can crushed pineapple, drained
2 cups carrots, grated
½ cup raisins
Frosting:
2 cups powdered sugar*
½ cup shortening*
2 tablespoons rice milk
1 teaspoon vanilla

In a large bowl or mixer, add flour, sugar, applesauce and rice milk; mix. Add baking powder, baking soda, salt, cinnamon, cloves, nutmeg, vinegar and vanilla; mix. Add shredded carrots, pineapple and raisins; stir. Pour into a greased 8-inch baking pan.
Bake at 350 degrees for 40 minutes.
Frosting: mix powdered sugar, shortening, rice milk and vanilla. Whip until fluffy. Spread on cooled cake.
*See baking tips, page 17

Oatmeal Raisin Cookies
Makes approximately 3 dozen cookies

2½ cups oat flour*
½ cup white sugar
½ cup brown sugar
½ cup applesauce
½ cup shortening
1 teaspoon ground cinnamon
½ teaspoon nutmeg
½ teaspoon baking soda
1 teaspoon baking powder*
½ teaspoon salt*
1 tablespoon apple cider vinegar
1 teaspoon vanilla
2 cups rolled oats
1 cup raisins

In a large bowl or mixer, add flour, sugar, brown sugar, applesauce and shortening; mix. Add cinnamon, nutmeg, baking soda, baking powder, salt, vinegar and vanilla; mix well. On low speed, add oats and raisins. Drop dough by rounded tablespoons onto a baking sheet.

Bake at 350 degrees for 13 minutes. Let cool on baking sheet for 5 minutes before removing.

Try replacing the raisins with semi-sweet chocolate chips!

*See baking tips, page 17

Crispy Cookies
Makes approximately 3 dozen cookies

3 cups oat flour*
1 cup sugar
½ cup brown sugar
1 cup shortening*
½ cup water
1 teaspoon baking soda
1 teaspoon baking powder*
1 teaspoon salt
2 teaspoons apple cider vinegar
1 teaspoon vanilla
2 cups rolled oats
2 cups rice crispy type cereal

In a large bowl or mixer, add flour, sugar, brown sugar and shortening; mix. Add water, baking soda, baking powder, salt, vinegar and vanilla; mix well. On low speed, add rolled oats and crispy cereal. Drop dough by rounded tablespoons onto a cookie sheet.

Bake for 13 minutes at 350. Let cool on baking sheet for 5 minutes before removing.

*See baking tips, page 17

Snickerdoodles
Makes approximately 3 dozen cookies

3½ cups oat flour*
¾ cup sugar
¼ cup brown sugar
½ cup shortening*
½ cup applesauce
1 teaspoon baking powder*
¼ teaspoon nutmeg
1 teaspoon cream of tarter
1 teaspoon baking soda
¼ teaspoon salt*
1 teaspoon vinegar
Cinnamon sugar topping:
1 tablespoon cinnamon
2 tablespoons sugar

In a large bowl or mixer, add flour, sugar, brown sugar, shortening and applesauce; mix. Add baking powder, nutmeg, cream of tarter, baking soda, salt and vinegar; mix well.

Cinnamon sugar topping: in a small bowl, combine cinnamon and sugar.

Drop dough by rounded tablespoons into cinnamon sugar and roll until well covered.

Bake at 350 for 13 minutes. Let cool on cookie sheet for 5 minutes before removing.

*See baking tips, page 17

Chocolate Oat Butter Cookies
Makes approximately 3 dozen cookies

2 cups sugar
½ cup shortening*
4 tablespoons cocoa powder
½ cup rice milk
½ cup sunflower seed butter
1 teaspoon vanilla
¼ teaspoon salt*
2 cups rolled oats

In a saucepan, add sugar, shortening, cocoa powder and rice milk; stir. Bring to a boil for one minute over medium high heat. Remove from heat and add sunflower seed butter; stir until melted in. Add vanilla, salt and oats; stir. Drop by rounded tablespoons onto waxed paper or cookie sheet and let cool.

*See baking tips, page 17

Chocolate-Butter Rice Bars
Makes approximately 3 dozen bars

1 cup sugar
1 cup rice syrup
1 cup sunflower seed butter
6 cups rice crispy type cereal
Topping:
2 cups semi-sweet chocolate chips*
1 tablespoon canola oil

In a saucepan, add sugar and rice syrup; bring to a light boil; remove from heat. Add sunflower seed butter; stir until melted in. Add rice crispy cereal; mix well. Press bar mixture into a greased 9 x 13 inch pan.

Topping: pour chocolate chips and oil into a medium size microwave safe dish. Put in the microwave on high for one minute; stir. Continue heating and stirring until chocolate is melted. Spread the melted mixture over the bar mixture. Allow topping to set before cutting.

These are great bars to bring to a party!

*See baking tips, page 17

Carmel Rice Puffs

6 cups puffed rice
2 tablespoons canola oil
1 cup brown sugar
½ cup rice syrup
½ teaspoon salt*
1 teaspoon baking soda

Place rice puffs in a well-greased 9 x 13 inch baking pan and set aside. In a medium size saucepan combine oil, brown sugar, rice syrup and salt. Over medium high heat, bring the sauce to a boil, stirring constantly for two minutes. Remove from heat and stir in baking soda, which will cause mixture to foam. Pour mixture over the rice puffs and stir until puffs are well covered.

Bake at 250 degrees for 10 minutes. Remove, stir and place back into oven for another 10 minutes. Remove, stir and let cool.

Scrape the leftover caramel off the sides of the saucepan and drop button sized pieces onto foil. This makes caramel candies!

*See baking tips, page 17

Flour-less Butter Cup Melts
Makes approximately 3 dozen cookies

1 cup sunflower seed butter
½ cup brown sugar
½ teaspoon baking soda
¼ teaspoon salt*
1 tablespoon apple cider vinegar
1 cup semi-sweet chocolate chips

In a mixing bowl, combine sunflower seed butter, brown sugar, baking soda, salt and vinegar; mix well. Stir in chocolate chips. Drop by rounded tablespoons onto a baking sheet.

Bake at 350 for 10 minutes.

Let cookies cool for at least 5 minutes before removing from sheet, they are very fragile!

These cookies literally melt in your mouth!

*See baking tips, page 17

Fruit and Sorbet Smoothie

1-2 servings

1 cup frozen strawberries
½ cup lemon sorbet
1 cup orange juice or rice milk

In a blender, add strawberries, sorbet and liquid;
blend. Add more liquid as needed for desired
thickness. Blend until smooth.

Frozen Juice Cubes or Popsicles

Organic lemonade or limeade

Pour juice into ice cube tray or popsicle mold and set in the freezer until frozen. Pop cubes out of tray or mold and serve.

This old-fashioned treat is healthy, easy and tastes refreshingly good! My children choose them over store bought popsicles every time!

Chocolate Frosting

1 cup powdered sugar*
½ cup cocoa
½ cup shortening*
1 teaspoon vanilla
4 tablespoons rice milk

In a medium size bowl or mixer, whip powdered sugar, cocoa, shortening, vanilla and rice milk for approximately 5 minutes, or until light and fluffy.

For a glossier frosting, whip in 1 tablespoon rice syrup.

For vanilla frosting, omit cocoa and add 1 cup powdered sugar.

Lemon Glaze Icing

½ cup sugar
¼ cup lemon juice
2 teaspoons grated lemon peel

In a saucepan, add sugar, lemon juice and lemon peel; bring to a boil. Remove from heat and drizzle glaze over cake immediately.

*See baking tips, page 17

Index

A

B

Artichoke Rice Salad, 66
Basil Rice, 59
Caramel Rice Puffs, 101
Chinese Rice, 58
Ground Turkey and Rice, 42
Spicy Beans and Rice, 56
"SB&J" Rice Cakes, 86
Rice Bread "Tortilla Chips", 80
S
Salad Dressings
French Dressing, 77
Italian Dressing, 77
Poppy Seed Dressing, 78
Salads
Black Bean Salad, 69
Coleslaw, 67
Cranberry Jello, 75
Fruit Salad, 73
Quinoa Salad, 68
Sesame Chicken Salad, 36
Sparkling Lemon-Lime Jello, 74
Spinach Salad, 71
Sweet and Sour Poppy Seed Salad, 72
Three Bean Salad, 70
Salsa, 82
Salsa, Peach, 83
Shopping List, 19
Smoothies
Strawberry Banana Smoothie, 28
Fruit and Sorbet Smoothie, 103
Soups
Barley and Beef Soup, 52
Beef Soup, 49